Heart-lifting Moments

Joyce Hill

First published in 2010
Copyright © 2010 Autumn House Publishing (Europe) Ltd

British Library Cataloguing in Publication Data.
A catalogue record for this book is
available from the British Library.

ISBN 978-1-906381-73-8

Published by Autumn House (Europe) Ltd.,
Grantham, Lincolnshire.
Designed by Abigail Murphy
Printed in Thailand.

My Friend

'I've found a Friend, oh, such a Friend!
He loved me ere I knew him;
He drew me with the cords of love.
And thus he bound me to him.
And round my heart still closely twine
Those ties which nought can sever,
For I am his, and he is mine,
For ever and for ever!'
James G. Small

Help with the chores?

Fridge magnets magnetise me. At least, the proliferation of them swinging on their stands in various shops does. Their pithiness, wit, dry humour – yes, even some of their banality – tickles my little grey cells into appreciative chuckles. Take this one, for example; it made me hoot with laughter.

'The only reason I have a kitchen is because it came with the house!'

How dumb can dumb blondes get!

But while the laughter was still dying on my lips, I realised that the truth behind the wit scratched me where so often I itch. I love those beautiful fitted kitchens, with all the mod cons, filling the pages of glossy magazines. But when it comes to the reality of my kitchen, that's a different story, because I don't really love getting into it. And I'm pretty certain that I'm not alone in this.

It's true I admire women who enjoy their kitchens and find fulfilment in them. Yet I can always think of a dozen things I'd rather do than plunge my hands into hot, detergenty water, get out the chopping board and cooking utensils, or scrub kitchen floors. Fortunately my mother made sure that I knew how to do all this, and more, while my mind and my body were still flexible.

How does one turn unfavourite chores into bearable, or even pleasant times? My endurance of duty has even become pleasurable because a good Friend comes to chat with me while I work. Would you like to eavesdrop?

Kitchens

The kitchen that came with my flat was new. It was also very empty. Oh, it had the usual basic sink, hot and cold taps and draining board, one miniscule work surface topped and bottomed with a couple of small cupboards, one disappointingly basic electric oven, a gas hob, and a whole blank wall. In fact, the basic 'one person flat' kitchen.

The size of the kitchen is actually a bonus. When I stand in the middle almost everything is within reach. The window is a joy, too. It's placed for sunshine to flood the kitchen from dawn until dusk, over-spilling into the living room. The light and the warmth are a continual joy.

Unpacking boxes when moving in – well, that was a pointless exercise. There was no place to put their contents! It took time, patience and a skilled carpenter to create a practical working/storage area in that empty, new kitchen.

It was still a challenge to try to fit all the contents of the boxes into the new cupboards. They had been stored in cupboards of a much larger kitchen, of course! Keeping old favourite utensils and discarding others – now that really left no room for sentiment.

Keeping . . . discarding . . . choices! So
much may be packed away in the boxes
of our minds during the daily hurly-
burley – everything from trash to
treasure. Before moving into a restful
night's sleep, it's a good idea to sift
through the collection of the day,
file and pack the boxes more carefully
for ease of future access.

That's the best of times, just my Friend
and I, storing the joys and soothing the
sorrows of the past hours, ready to move
into a new day – if not a new kitchen.

Food, glorious food!

Cookery books

Most kitchens have a stash of cookbooks somewhere about, and this kitchen that came with the house is no exception. Aren't they just the stuff that dreams are made of? The colourful glossiness of the step-by-step illustrations set the saliva glands working, even before you read the list of ingredients.

•

Now we all know and love two kinds of
cooks . . . maybe more, but chiefly two.
There's the dedicated culinary artiste,
who follows the recipe to the last grain of
sugar and who wobbles the scales to the
very last milligram of flour. She also
stirs, beats, folds and adds ingredients
according to the instructions, preheating
the oven to the correct temperature.

Then there is the talented, widely
experienced cook who has no time for
cookbooks. Such a cook will toss a
handful of this, a pinch of that, a lump of
something or other, and a walnut-sized
piece of that into a good ol' yellow mixing
bowl, whisk away with a most
dexterously neat turn of the wrist,
before sliding the mixture into a well-
prepared tin. The dish is then slid into a
hot oven – usually middle shelf – and
the oven door closed upon it. When the
cooked dishes are placed side by side on
the table, it would take an expert
to judge which is the better.

I guess people are like those cooks. Some of us need to refer to the book to improve our methods and find new ideas, or just to give us confidence. Others are so familiar with cooking that 'the basics' are in their minds and hearts. Both kinds serve tasteful food, and when their results are seen, who is to say that one is better than the other?

You know, of course, that our Friend in the Kitchen's own recipe book is the world's bestseller? It's full of splendid ideas for healthy, happy living. It makes the best of bedtime reading, too!

It's a great favourite with me.

14

A bread-maker recipe

Ingredients	Amount
Water of life	as to quench thirst
Honey of commitment	as duty requires
Oil of gladness	generous splash
Word of life flour	studied amount
Word of truth flour	wholesome mindful
Sweetness of genuine love	unselfish heart-full
(Dried) Milk of human kindness	2 generous handfuls
Salt of humour	a discreet sprinkling
Yeast of the Holy Spirit	according to his will

Method

Place ingredients as listed into bread-maker. Set to moderate temperature. Cook until loaf is Son-kissed in colour, and a gentle tap sounds like 'Use me!'

Message from my Friend in the Kitchen

All the ingredients for this recipe are available from my Libra Sanctum Supermarket. They are always fresh, and need no 'Use by' date. To anyone who asks to be served by me personally, all goods are free. Just ask for me. . . .

Jesus

Herbs and spices

They are so interesting, those
shelves of spices in the supermarket –
saffron and cinnamon, nutmeg and
mace, cumin, curry, cardamom and
cloves. Not far away are shelves of
potted herbs, all fresh, green and ripe for
picking – parsley, bay leaves, mint, sage,
chives and oregano, to name but a few.

Many spices are well travelled.
Remember the old Silk Road climbing
across the Roof of the World, linking
traders in silks, spices and more, with
the Far East and Europe? Thrilling tales
that are much more exciting to read
about than to experience.

Such thoughts of wearisome travel drive me to my armchair. Reading Ellis Peter's description of Cadfael's herbarium at Shrewsbury Abbey back in the twelfth century is much more relaxing. The aromatic delight of those sun-warmed herbs and spices in the lit garden twilight is a heady dream.

Here in this 'green and pleasant land' supermarkets trawl the world to keep our food well flavoured. We have little idea of the struggle people had in earlier centuries to survive cold winters without starving. Herbs and spices were important as preservatives. They were essential for disguising the taste of stale, unappetising meat and fish as winter took its hold. It's fascinating to read about the banquets held in palaces and stately homes, and to picture the richly dressed guests clutching spicy posies to ward off unpleasant aromas.

A pinch of spice or a sprig of herbs adds piquancy to food. How we enjoy the varied flavours! In our home, before we begin to eat, we look to our Friend and thank him for this meal. Sometimes he reminds us of faraway places, of hard-working people, of production lines, transportation and storage, all of which contribute to the food on our plates.

It's by his constant grace that harvests ripen and their produce is brought to market. It is by his loving goodness that we are able to buy food for our needs.

Can we ever thank him enough for his bounty?

Homemade stew

Peel and chop onion (any size that's
handy). In a splash of olive oil sauté with
mushrooms while preparing carrot,
swede, celery (and anything else you
fancy) to create a family stew. Add a
pint or so of vegetable stock (a crumbled
stock cube is quick and easy). Stir well,
and when on a rolling boil add potato
flour mixed in water to thicken. Add
herbs (salt if you must) to taste.
Simmer with one eye on the clock while
finding your shoes.

Pour this into a slow cooker (not your shoes), pull on your jacket, grab the car keys – and run. You're late! Open the car door, slam it, dash back into the kitchen and check you've switched on the slow cooker. Cast a disgusted look at the cluttered kitchen, shout up the stairs, 'Clear up the kitchen for me, dear! I haven't got time.' Slam two more doors, crash the gears, kangaroo hop a yard or two, and you're off and away.

There you have it – a recipe for stew. Or is it two recipes? There are several types of stew recipes to be found in cookbooks, and there are several other kinds of stews in life that we get thrown into. Or should that be 'jump into'? The non-food kind comes in various flavours, such as emotional, relational, intellectual, bad timing, misunderstanding, stupidity, stubbornness, jealousy, accidental, mistakenly, as well as, and including, your own scenario.

'Now what,' you demand in your distress, 'is your Friend in the Kitchen going to do about **this** stew?'

Firstly, he'll encourage you to remember that he is **your** Friend, too. Secondly, he'll remind you that he is with you in dark moments and always loves you. He may see fit to apply a cold compress to ease your strain and pain. But his hands are gentle. If you look into his face you will see compassion. If you talk to him you will find your tension released. If you listen to him you will find solutions.

Your heart will be comforted.

You will find peace.

Mushrooms

Time for a tasty snack, and I was peeling mushrooms when a surprised voice attacked me. 'Why are you peeling those mushrooms? I never do.'

Quick reply: 'I always peel my mushrooms!' True, I did always peel them, but it wasn't until giving it more thought that the real answer occurred to me. I always peel mushrooms because my mother did.

Mushrooms were found in fields, not shops, when we were young. They were a treat that we youngsters harvested from the fields around our home – fields that were shared with cows or sheep or horses. So my mother peeled those mushrooms because, as she said, 'You never know where they've been!' Today mushrooms are cultivated in climate and hygienically controlled conditions. Their creamy whiteness merely needs a quick wipe and a few cuts with a knife before they are ready for the pan.

I began to wonder how many other habits of mine are rooted in the things my mother taught me; probably far more than I can remember or care to share. So much of who we are today is the sum total of what we imbibed from our parents and their lifestyle. Sometimes we hear it expressed by folk who say, 'What was good enough for my parents is good enough for me.'

It's true that the above statement is used in reference to 'the faith of their fathers'. But I believe that my parents' faith is not good enough for me! I'm grateful that my siblings and I were raised in a committed Christian home, but my parents' faith was not mine. It was my mother's faith, my father's faith, in a living God. Their encouragement and prayers showed me the way to go to find my own faith, my own personal relationship with a loving Saviour.

It's that personal faith of mine that brings joy to both of us when my heavenly Friend meets me in the kitchen.

Sauce

A magnet on my fridge reads, 'Many people have eaten food from this kitchen and gone on to lead normal healthy lives.' Now that's something to be extremely grateful for. Not only so, happy times were shared, too. That's not to say that everything was always perfect, for finished dishes do not always live up to the expectations of the cook.

It's amazing what a cook can do with 'mistakes', bland dishes and/or what's-left-in-the-pantry, with a dollop of sauce. It can make all the difference to a dish, either savoury or sweet. So much choice of sauces too – shelves of them in the supermarkets, recipe books full of them on the bookshelves (and in my kitchen), and enough ingenuity in most cooks in the kitchen to create their own brand.

Homemade is best of course – just a drizzle of oil, some onion, tomato, herbs, and the rest is up to what you fancy . . . oh, and a touch of garlic. Some after-meal mints might be helpful here! Or just think how chocolate sauce can turn a plain ice cream into a luscious luxury!

Our rich and fruitful English language can take sauce from the pan and pour it out as a word – **sauciness**. As sauce adds piquancy to a dish, so sauciness adds piquancy to a situation. A little sauciness can be fun at the right time. It can be cleverly witty. If used indiscreetly it may be embarrassing, unsocial or downright rude. Over-spilled sauces leave stubborn stains on the cloth. Over-indulged sauciness leaves stains on the heart.

Our Friend in the Kitchen has always advised a simple, natural diet for a healthy life. Sauces are fine sometimes, but fattening always. A touch of sauciness may be amusing, but not always gracious. Simple, gracious speech is what our Friend is listening for.

That's his kind of language – ever truthful, ever graceful.

Tomatoes

Versatile – that's a fine word for tomatoes, don't you think? You may be served tomatoes and mushrooms with (or without) a good old English breakfast, tomato soup and/or a variety of dishes using tomatoes at lunchtime, then add to that the variety of sauces and tomato dishes that are served for dinner. Remember salads, picnics, sandwiches, pizzas and quiches . . . you've got the idea. And please don't forget tomato chutney!

These days, tomatoes are in supermarkets all through the year, as suppliers follow seasonal growth around the world. Even better, many keep their kitchens supplied with home-grown varieties that have been raised in greenhouses, gardens, patio tubs or grow-bags. They really taste so good.

I have read of people keeping to a diet overflowing with tomatoes as a cure for cancer. They are certainly full of goodness and tasty with it. Recently a snippet in a newspaper's food column attracted my attention. It stated various health benefits from eating tomatoes but added that the full benefit of one amino acid in particular (lysine) is not achieved unless tomatoes are heated at some point before eating. Lysine is necessary for the building of proteins and production of enzymes, hormones and antibodies. Lysine helps clear up cold sores, too.

The tastiest tomatoes are those that are grown where they are warmed in natural sunlight. The lovely deep crimson colour, the particular aroma of ripe tomatoes, provide a pleasant picture as well as being a pleasure to the palate.

'And that,' suggests my Friend in the Kitchen, 'is just where you grow best, too. Son-bathing in the warmth of the Father's love, absorbing his goodness as you cling to the vine, letting your special fragrance fill the air around you.'

Even if we accept that advice we will never grow into tomatoes.

But we will be filled with the fruit of the Spirit.

Water

'Water, water everywhere – nor any drop to drink!' said the Ancient Mariner, alone on the deck of his becalmed ship.

'Water, water everywhere! Now which brand of bottled water shall I drink?' I misquote while roaming along the tiers of shelves in the supermarket.

The Ancient Mariner had no choice. Drinking seawater would have made him sick to death. Here in the supermarket there is a huge choice. Could it be that the wrong choice could make me sick to death, too?

Recently an article in a national newspaper addressed this bottled water business. It highlighted both dangers and benefits, and there were sensible and believable arguments for and against. With that article in mind, the bottled waters were left on the shelves and I went home to a glass of filtered tap water.

Tap water in this area is hard. It leaves lime-scale in all the places it runs through or over. So there's a water filter in constant use in my kitchen. The filtered water tastes no different from tap water, but some of us feel better drinking water that has been drained through a healthy, charcoal filter.

Keeping water pure is big business and requires constant vigilance from water authorities. When earthquakes, tsunamis or hurricanes devastate an area, one of the first concerns of relief agencies is to supply drinking water. Water is life. Without it we die.

Our Friend in the Kitchen has many names by which he is known. One of them is the 'Water of Life'. He reminds us that to find a life full of joy, of utter fulfilment, we need to drink the pure water from his fountain. He longs to quench our thirst from his showers of grace. With him there are no droughts, no bottled water, no opening or closing times. So why not drink – and be refreshed?

That cake

A special day, special guests, special cake to cook. No problem – that is until the cake came out of the oven. It smelled good and it looked good – except that the middle of the cake had collapsed. Tragedy! How did that happen? Someone slammed the kitchen door during cooking time. Oh dear, now what?

Mistakes happen. No one **meant** to slam the door when the cake was in the oven. 'He who never made a mistake never made anything.' Platitudes roll easily off the tongue: 'Mistakes are stepping stones to success.' Comforting, but not exactly helpful on this occasion. However, given time for the cook and the cake to cool down, the mistake was easily rectified.

The top of the cake was sliced off, giving the cake a level surface. Now the sliced-off top looked like a circle. A covering of glacé icing for the bottom half of the cake, and a powdering of icing sugar over the circle quite disguised the accident. Decorated with almond halves and glacé cherries the round cake became almost a triumph, while the ring looked equally delectable filled with a few berries.

Once more that fridge magnet in my kitchen, 'All mistakes guaranteed edible', proved true.

My Friend who meets me in the kitchen
reminds me that he is often
busy turning around mistakes and
accidents, even covering them up.
Sometimes we must suffer the
consequences of our own folly, but even
then his love bandages our wounds if we
will accept his help. Sometimes it seems
as though our Friend twists and turns
circumstances to help us wriggle out of
the enemy's traps. But always, always,
he knows and cares when we mess up.
He longs to put things right, to wipe the
slate clean for everyone. Everyone
includes me – and you!

We only need to ask him.

Give me the tools

Glass tumblers

Question: When does a tumbler become a drinking glass?

Or conversely: When should a drinking glass be called a tumbler?

A touch of Googling got me nowhere, except perhaps a suggestion that tumblers may be shorter than drinking glasses, and they prefer holding whisky to soft drinks. What is certain is that drinking glasses appear and disappear with unerring regularity in many a kitchen, for glass is fragile.

Glass is as old as sweltering sunshine and searing desert sands. Now it is a vast industry, manufacturing huge, unbreakable sheets down to the tiniest sparkling ornaments. But it's the super-skilled glassblowers who magnetise me.

There's a fascinating Glass Works tourist attraction way down in the southwest of England. Bunkers of different kinds of sand lie near to a row of furnaces. In a huge space in front of the furnaces brawny men wield their long pipes, blowing controlled air into globules of molten glass. It's intriguing to watch so many different shapes and sizes grow on the end of that long pipe.

Yet, sadly, even the most skilled workman can make a mistake, or see his glass globule's shape collapse. All he can do then is to shake the spoiled glass off the blowpipe and begin again.

From time to time all the wasted, broken glass is swept up and tipped back into the fiery furnace. It's called **cullet**. Reheated and liquefied cullet is reshapable.

My Friend knows all too well that we human beings are as fragile as glass and frequently tumble into trouble. He sees our mistakes and feels our brokenness. Isn't it comforting to know that always he's ready to sweep us into the warmth of his love, happy to shape us into beautiful, useful people, each one a shining, unique design?

Let's raise our glasses in a toast of love and gratitude to our redemptive Friend and Lord . . . and feel his smile!

Golden Jubilee

Some days really are special, and this
Silver Jubilee morning was one of them.
This morning King George V and Queen
Mary were to drive past our house.
We would see them clearly. This
afternoon all the children of the borough
were to have a celebration party in the
beautiful town park.

Wow!

So it happened. My family hung out of our high-up windows, watching the crowds. A ripple of cheering grew to a roar. Flags waved as the royal coach passed by. King George and Queen Mary sat so upright, so regal, smiling and waving to the crowds lining the road. Slowly and steadily plumed horses pulled the coach onwards. The cheering roar lessened to a ripple, and the coach was gone. The crowds moved away. That was the end of the royal progress. That was the end of the morning. It was the beginning of the afternoon.

Party time came. Crowds of schoolchildren passed through the park gates to their appointed places. First, there was a speech from the mayor. As he stood on a platform with wooden steps leading up to it, one boy and one girl, representing each school, walked up those wooden steps and each was given a silver spoon by the mayor. On the spoon was a little gold medallion that had King George and Queen Mary's heads on it. The date was there, too. That's how I happen to have a Silver Jubilee teaspoon in my kitchen drawer. The mayor gave it to me and shook my hand. I still treasure it.

That Silver Jubilee excitement pales at the thought of a Royal Visit soon to come. Our Friend will arrive as King of all kings. The glory that attends him will be beyond description. There will be trumpets, shouts of joy and clouds of glorious attendants. He brings no silver teaspoons, but flight to an idyllic homeland. We shall have new names, crowns of gold and hearts overflowing with love for our Sovereign Lord. He longs for us all to be waiting for his arrival.

Are **you** waiting?

Kettles

'What is the most essential piece of equipment you need for your Mums and Toddlers' club?' the leader asked.

This was the opening gambit to a group of ladies attending a course on the dos and don'ts of running toddler groups. After a short silence, a confident voice declared, 'A kettle!' 'There speaks the voice of experience,' said the tutor. 'A hot cuppa for the mums to drink will help to generate a relaxed attitude, . . .' and she was away into her subject.

The kettle is certainly a part of our social graces, from the one heated by the car cigarette lighter to the big urn that forever flows for large functions. 'Would you like a nice warm drink?' – isn't that one of the first questions we ask friends and guests when they visit? And the kettle in the ward kitchen of a hospital is put to good use on many a sleepless night.

So please raise your teacups to kettles!

Our family kettle was big and black. It sat, always filled, on the hob of the stove in our kitchen. It was all ready for action. My kitchen is rather hankering after a 'watch-the-bubbles-while-I-boil' type. It would be more interesting to see it boil.

Kettles, like us, come in all shapes and sizes, from tin to iron to copper, polished stainless steel and even glass. The advert says of the glass ones, '. . . so that you can see the bubbles!' As long as kettles hold water and can stand heat, they are welcome in the kitchen. These days they are welcome in many bedrooms, too.

My Friend in the Kitchen sometimes tells me I'm like a kettle – not a lot of use just sitting there. I need filling with water from his well. I need heating with his love to make me hot enough for use. I need his watchful care to stop me 'blowing my lid' and filling the air with steam. Then in the right time and place he is able to pour me out to bring restorative comfort to a thirsting soul.

You, too?

Microwaves

What amazingly electrifying changes occurred during the last hundred years! From horse-drawn buses to tube trains, from air balloons to rockets . . . and from black kitchen ranges to chrome microwave ovens. Wow! Neither does there seem any end to the inventions appearing all around us. Understandably, some have been more welcome than others. Some are even controversial with scientists and consumers alike.

Among such questioned commodities in the kitchen is the microwave oven. It's popular, easy to use and, best of all, speedy. It's unpopular with folk who refuse to use it because a) they don't understand it and fear it; b) they believe it to be radioactive and therefore dangerous; c) they have genuine scientific reservations about the wisdom of its use in preparing food for human consumption.

As merely the domestic in the kitchen that came with this house I'm neither competent nor willing to debate any of the above. My microwave is a lifesaver from labour, stress and the clock's incessant ticking. More simply put, I like it, enjoy it, and bless its inventor.

I guess the popularity of microwave cooking lies in its faster cooking/reheating times. That, surely, is a reflection on the lives so many of us live these days. Striding from quick to hurry to rush to stress to burnout, without our microwaves we could well become undernourished.

If we are truly honest, we'll admit that food cooked in the microwave is not really as tasty as when cooked more conventionally. Something is missing in food whose molecules have been so speedily disturbed. Slower cooking certainly has flavoursome advantages.

A gentle nudge from our Friend right here
in the kitchen reminds me that there's
quite a relationship between fast micro
cooking and our friendship with him.
Spending a little longer with him during
the day will surely improve the flavour of
our friendship, and add colour that
'microwave' visiting never will.

He'd love that!

Left-handedness

It's been said many a time – surely
you've heard it – that 'left-handed
people are the only ones in their right
minds'. Scientists are working on it;
they've even found a gene for it – left-
handedness, that is. Statistics say that
the number of left-handed people has
tripled over the last century. They also
think more quickly and are better at
learning languages. With such
advantages, it almost makes one wish to
be left-handed.

But not quite, for there is a dearth of kitchen implements and tools to be found for use of such people in the kitchen! I've found a drum food-grater and some laser scissors, which are truly for left-handed cooks, but most gadgets are described as 'for L and R users'.

Imagine a left-handed woman trying to teach a right-handed person to knit or sew or write – or cook! Perhaps not, if you stress easily! I'm so glad that the days of 'persuading' left-handed children to use their right hands are gone. That was very tough, even harmful to young brains.

Not having a scientific understanding of the brain's activities has never been a barrier to a left-hander's progress. Those little grey cells go on working whether you are conscious of them or not. Generations past and present have lived left-handed yet full, rich and enjoyable lives. Many have become famous artists, musicians, sportsmen, executives, even presidents of countries.

There aren't any left-handed gadgets in my kitchen. They're not important. What is important is that my friends are welcome in my kitchen; that I neither know nor care whether they're left-handed, right-handed or ambidextrous. They're my friends and welcome. What's truly important is that my Friend in the Kitchen holds out his hands to me, to you, to everybody, reminding us by nail marks in both his right hand and his left, that his love is utterly inclusive – and forever.

Pots and pans

Isn't it interesting how coming across a
word or phrase will lead to a new thought
or a vivid memory? That's what 'pots
and pans' does to me. I see a horse
drawing a colourful cart hung about
with tin pots, pans, colanders and every
kind of tin ware. The travelling tinker
was a welcome sight to villagers
of years gone by.

How different are the kitchen departments of superstores today. We find pots and pans manufactured from colourful cast iron, copper, glass and stainless steel. There may even be some of the above with heat-retaining aluminium sandwiched in the base. There are those with/without lids, with/without handles, or clip-on handles. You'll find milk pans, saucepans, frying pans, chef's pans, omelette pans and non-stick pans. There are porringers and bains-marie, slow cookers, woks, stockpots and crock-pots . . . the list goes on.

There are two factors common to every variety of pot or pan. They are made for use, and to withstand high temperatures. Without these qualities pans are of no value to the cook. Neither does kitchenware have any choice as to how it is used or abused.

Do you see that we share these two factors as well? We are created to be filled and to serve, to bear the heat of life's stresses. But, unlike pots and pans, we can make choices. Circumstances may have a strong influence on our lives, yet we have the freedom to choose whether we will stay 'in the kitchen' with our Friend, or whether we will get out. Our choices will determine whether we develop characters of cast iron or stainless steel, or whether we become slow cookers or crock-pots.

Our Friend is a wonderful counsellor. We don't have to make an appointment to ask for his advice. He has the experience and ability to help us cope with anything that life throws at us. He knows how to turn down the heat when we boil over. We can ask him to watch over us, or we can get out of the kitchen.

The choice is yours. Choose wisely.

Mother's knife

My cutlery drawer contains, among a
variety of kitchen flotsam, three bone-
handled, stainless steel knives. They are
all useful, but one is special. That's
because it was my mother's favourite
table knife and, somehow, sometime, it
landed in my kitchen drawer.

It will be no surprise to learn that all three knives were made in the heart of the steel industry, Sheffield, city on seven hills. Two of those three knives, at first glance, seem identical. The pattern of the steel where it joins the bone is identical. The handles and the blades are the same size and shape. But they increase in interest as the etching on the blade is examined. Each knife is manufactured by a different Sheffield company. One is labelled 'Firth Stainless' from James Walker Steel Works, the second reads 'Firth's Stainless' from Dawes and Ball Cutlery Manufacturers, and the third, 'Firth Brearly' Stainless – Warranted Stainless Steel, Sheffield.

A brief chat with erudite Yahoo is enlightening here. Harry Brearly was a scientist who specialised in improving stainless steel, while Thomas Firth and Sons were leading manufacturers of steel. When Brearly joined Firth and Sons in post World War 1, stainless steel began to flourish, becoming the polished and sharp commodity that it is today.

The curiosity to learn the age of my mother's table knife has now found some satisfaction. It is very likely ninety-five years old. It may look like the other bone handled knives, yet when looked at more closely it is recognisably different. Recognising the differences, that this is my mother's favourite, I reach for this knife first.

Just as I am one of a myriad human beings with a unique DNA, and useful for my own special gifts and personality, so are you. So are we all! As with Mother's knife, age will not reduce our value or purpose. Rather, given time, a keener edge and a mirror-polish, we shall become part of a shining exhibition to a vast, eternal universe.

Those teaspoons

I'm washing dishes, and my brain slips into stand-by mode.

I read a humorous article once, entitled, 'Why is there always a teaspoon left in the bottom of the washing-up bowl?' Huh? I thought, and took special notice when washing my dishes over the next few days. Sure enough, my teaspoons played hide-and-seek with me enough times to prove the point. In fact, they still catch me out once in a while, and still make me chuckle while giving the culprit a hot shower.

I haven't a clue how **laws of average** and **left-behind teaspoons** compare, combine or contrast, but I do know that the 'left behind' phrase really grabbed my attention. My mind's eye saw a group of children running through flower-studded fields, a tiny tot way behind crying, 'Wait for meeeeee!' Scary!

It's a sad fact that too many people get left behind, sinking to the bottom of life's overflowing bowl. In moments of compassion we think of tragedies causing multitudes of reasons for homelessness and helplessness. Sadly we think of people, from babies to great-grandparents, who are subjected to neglect and abuse. Like the teaspoon, they need to be found and restored to their place.

This generation, our generation, has produced a group of people who are aware of being left behind. They are the lonely elderly who speak of family living in faraway places; those with no family who're alone for endless dreary hours and sleepless nights. You may have heard the sadness in the voice of an elderly relative or friend who tells you that all their contemporaries have died and, 'I'm the only one of my age left.' Not a comfortable feeling, for sure.

Now the dishes are done, the last
teaspoon clean and dry. An urgent
whisper escapes from my heart. 'Lord,
please don't leave me behind when you
come to take us home!'

Comes the whispered answer,
'My child, the choice is yours.'

Spatula

He was devastated, our next-door-but-
one neighbour, and no wonder, for he had
recently lost his wife. Frequently he
found his way into our kitchen to find
some comfort over a 'cuppa' and a chat.
He and my husband had the loss of a
loved one in common, and when Cecil
asked, as frequently he did, 'How did you
cope when . . .?' my husband always
replied, 'Keep busy, do anything you like,
but keep busy!'

Gradually we saw less of our neighbour for he disappeared into his little workshop under the back garden steps. He found solace in making two needlework boxes for his young granddaughters, and they were truly works of art. One day he arrived in our kitchen with a neatly made wooden mug holder and a wooden spatula. Useful gifts, simple gifts, but made especially for us in gratitude for our neighbourliness.

That was all of twenty years ago, yet still the spatula is in frequent use in this kitchen-that-came-with-the-house. So is the mug tree. I think of Cecil, his wife and the 'good old days' while using them both. I remember my husband's prescription for grief, 'Keep busy,' and have cause to be thankful for his advice.

Keeping your hands busy gives your mind a break from consuming sorrow, while giving time for healing. Cecil found that making gifts for his family opened a glimpse of the future that was waiting for him. He found satisfaction in working while he waited.

Maybe that's why we are in the kitchen.
We need to be busy using the tools that
are our gifts, often thinking of others,
anticipating a future brighter than the
turmoil this old world is enduring.

My Friend in the Kitchen says,
'Good idea. Occupy till I come. Keep
busy. Your future grows closer every
day, and it is very bright. I'm busy, too,
preparing a place for **you**.'

Silver

Don't you just love to gaze at a banqueting table laid out in all its glittering glory? Those proud and stately homes open to public viewing give us a glimpse of elegant dining. All that silver laid out just so, like shining soldiers stationary on parade. And so many of them! It's a dazzling but daunting sight to the uninitiated, but just in case you have forgotten how it's used, let me remind you. The dinner guest will begin with the outside silver and move inwards with the progression of each course of the meal. (At least, that's what my mother taught me.)

That shiny silver! Too precious to place in the dishwasher, each item is washed carefully by hand. It's dried equally carefully so as not to leave a spot of moisture on it. Then, and not infrequently, all this silver needs polishing – careful, painstaking polishing. To quote Shakespeare: 'Ay, there's the rub!' Rubbing and polishing take the gilt off owning real silverware!

There is an aspect of silver that intrigues me more than seeing it displayed in its glory in elegant surroundings. Before being fashioned into objets d'art, silver is rigorously refined. That's much more serious than a polishing rub. To do this, silver is placed in a crucible over great heat, and held there until it liquefies. The skill of the silversmith lies in knowing the exact moment when the silver is ready to be used. That moment is when the silversmith sees his own face perfectly reflected on the surface of the silver.

Our Friend is also a silversmith, and he refines us like precious silver. He, too, feels the heat of the furnace as he holds the crucible – the crucible of life – refining our characters. He watches to be sure that the temperature is neither too high nor too low. With patience he watches until he sees his own reflection in us. Then we, like silver, are beautifully crafted into a new creation. We have become exhibits of his love, each in our own niche.

And as the Son shines on us, so we shine for him.

Cleanliness is next to godliness

Bottoms up!

Don't you find it just a tad humiliating when your hands are immersed in that sudsy water, and your co-labourer returns a dish to be washed again? It can happen to any dishwasher, even the mechanical kind, I believe.

There we were, a friend and I, splashing away with the dishcloth and tea towel in a stranger's kitchen. On taking a pretty dinner plate out of the suds, we took one look at it and simultaneously said, 'Wow!' Bottom side up that plate looked as though it had never felt the gentle, or otherwise, touch of a dishcloth. But with a bit of tender loving care that plate, with all its fellows, was soon pristine once more.

The moment was quite a reminder. Like the proverbial pancake (and not forgetting the dinner plates), there are always, and at least, two sides to every question, no matter how thin those sides may be. The disabled owner of the pretty dinner service was only able to see one side, and that was pitiful. Back in my kitchen, tending my own dishes, I noticed some of the undersides of my plates were not as perfectly clean as they should be, and that was through just not paying attention.

Five minutes to do the dishes! A quick swish over the tops of plates, a wipe around the insides of beakers and cups, a short rinse, and that's the dishes done. Sometimes it's healthier to slow down and take a look at what is going on at 'the bottom of the plate' – underneath the superficiality of our lives. Sometimes it takes a bit of painful rubbing, even a touch of a cleansing agent before purity is restored.

My plates are clean now. My Good Friend is taking care of my life, topside and bottom-side, inside and outside. I have no need to fear a heavenly hygiene inspection. For that I'm glad, and praise him from the bottom of my heart.

Soaked

It's quite surprising, the topics covered when we women get together; everything from the National Health Service to baby's first tooth, or just women's plain wittering. Many a time the world has been put right over a 'cuppa' in the kitchen, offspring bragged or moaned about, holidays and romances fantasised about, and the law laid down as to the best brand of powder to use in the washing machine.

Then there's every housewife's best way of doing things, and if you don't agree then you will be wrong! This time it was how the kitchen is left at night. Evidently there are those of us who leave the bed-time mugs by the sink until the morning, There are others who leave the kitchen perfectly neat and tidy ready for a new day, and others (who are not of us) who leave the supper dishes soaking overnight. 'Ugh!' said a friend, ' I loathe putting my hands into cold, greasy water!' 'Put on your rubber gloves,' says another. 'It's soon tipped out, and you've got a head start on washing up.'

Facing up to a bowlful of cold, soaked dishes is certainly far from appealing, but there, it comes to all of us sometimes, and whether it's a couple of mugs, or dishes from a dinner party, it's a great feeling when the last dish is dried and the kitchen is back to rights.

You could imagine that this old world became as unwelcoming as a bowlful of greasy, messy dishes soaking in its own mucky environment. I can't think that it gave our Friend any pleasure to leave the joys of Heaven to plunge into such an unattractive situation as this. Yet he did, and it cost him dearly.

Even now he's cleaning and polishing. In the not too distant future the work will be done, and every item will be placed in the cupboard of his Kingdom. Never again will there be soaking in anything unpleasant or cold, just pristine cleanliness and golden glory evermore, for everyone.

Tea towels

'Don't let So-'n'-so dry the dishes. She always makes the towels wet!' the dishwasher said.

Oops!

Oddly enough, I thought that that's exactly what tea towels were for – to dry dishes and therefore to become wet. That's the reason my linen drawer holds an abundance of tea towels. I like to keep them on the move.

It's never been any problem to own a good supply of TTs. They make very acceptable gifts and are easy to pack in the 'going home from holiday' luggage. Some of them update a little history or geography of places near and far, some fill me with nostalgia, and some are so beautiful they ornament my kitchen door as works of art. What's more, they're all gifts, and therefore precious.

Sure, TTs get wet, collect germs that, rightly or wrongly, are the scourge of kitchens. I'm told they even have names that I don't intend to test on my spell checker. Instead, my tea towels are washed, dried (and even ironed) and put back into service.

My Friend who talks to me in the kitchen reminds me that he takes care of all his people in much the same way as we care for tea towels. When we're soaked with tears of grief and pain his words comfort us as he hangs us out to dry in the warm sunshine of his love. When we're all screwed up and messy after a difficult morning in a cluttered kitchen, we're washed, disinfected and cleansed by his forgiveness, and put back into service when he needs us.

That's what tea towels are for – service.

Rather like us,
don't you think?

Dishwashers

There was a time when I had a
dishwasher. My dishwasher was of the
very earliest kind. Created with the
finest and most delicate of components,
no task proved too difficult to handle.
Maintenance was no problem, and I
loved him. You see, my dishwasher was
my husband. Now I miss him – and not
just for the dish washing either!

A tabletop model of a dishwasher decorated my large kitchen during my husband's 'invalid' years. It was really too small, but coped with the endless stream of cups and mugs left behind when visitors passed through. A normal sized machine was too large for my needs, so for the most part there was nothing else to do but pull on my rubber gloves and plunge into hot water.

I'm sure dishwashers do a wonderfully hygienic and sparkling job, but when watching friends loading and unloading theirs, I wonder if they're really worth the expense and room. Surely it takes less time to use the bowl-in-the sink way than it does to do it the machine way? Doesn't it?

Silver cutlery and glassware are spoiled when put through a dishwasher. They thrive much better when cleaned individually in warm, sudsy water, dried, then finished off with a gentle polish.

Wiping each piece of cutlery separately, I'm reminded that people are like that. We can all do with a warm cleansing and a bit of a soothing polish. One of the very best of times for receiving such refreshing is at the close of day. Just relaxing in the hands of the best of friends, letting him wash away the hurts, feeling the soothing comfort of his hands – that's when we find peace and quietness for a while. That's when we're prepared to be useful again.

Stains

Maybe the only place where things stained are appreciated is in stained glass windows. Some of the beautiful, ancient, leaded ones are historical and national treasures. They are appreciated and enjoyed. Tea, coffee, wine and ketchup stains are not, definitely **not**, appreciated and enjoyed. In fact, cleaning up various stains in house and home creates big business these days. At least, that is what I assume, judging from the many and various cleaning agents advertised in kitchen catalogues.

I've picked up a solution or two for curing stains in my time. Haven't we all?

Washing machines and powders, even at 40° temperatures, will banish most everyday stains. Yet a drop or two of water on satin will leave unwelcome marks. Then there are special cases, like using surgical spirits to remove ink stains from shirts; sticky tape to lift lily-pollen stains from favourite jumpers, and saliva to clear (small) blood stains! A professional cleaner once said that if saliva could be synthesised it could put the cleaning trade out of business. Now there's a thought!

We all of us enjoy pristine purity in our household linen and our clothing. It feels good, it looks good and it's healthy. It takes an observant eye, time and effort to produce – even more time and effort for stubborn stains. But it's worth it.

Here, my Friend in the Kitchen reminds me that staining occurs in our living as well as in our clothing. The thoughts that drop into our minds so easily, the sights that flash before our eyes, the feelings that throb our hearts; they need observing, too, lest by carelessness we are stained by temptations of the world. The close of the day is a good time to relax with our Friend, talk with him, allow him to check for any spills, accept his cleansing from wear and tear of the past hours, and be refreshed.

Amazingly, his perfect cleansing agent is an oxymoron. It is his blood, applied with heartfelt love, and it washes whiter than snow.

Recycling

All good gardeners do it. Country folk
always have done it. This eco-green
population is encouraged to do it.
Recently a large, bright red ceramic apple
arrived in my kitchen, so now I do it.
Create compost, that is.

Once, all household waste went in the
dustbin, and very few of us knew or
cared where it went afterwards. Now we
know. It's a place called 'landfill', and
we're warned that landfill is running out.

Now, instead of stuffing vegetable trimmings and leftovers into plastic wrapping and then the dustbin, my kitchen waste lands in the core of my big fat apple, where a special biodegradable lining appreciates it. This will, in turn, reach a communal compost site, where it will become part of the nitrogen cycle and a happy hunting ground for worms.

Waste is certainly a huge problem. This throwaway generation provides a multiplicity of it. Recycling is a great way of coping with it. Charity shops, church sales, car boot sales are just a few ways of reminding us that some people's waste is someone else's treasure. Some people even make a good living through recycling services.

Everything that passes into that
'kitchen which came with the house'
needs re-appraisal, sooner or later.
Unnecessary wrappings, overripe fruit,
worn-out stuff, require sorting into
suitable receptacles: tins, glass, plastic,
cardboard, compost – whatever.

It's not just stuff that needs recycling or
dumping. What about that plethora of
stuff that continually enters your head?
How about those emotions that soothe
or ruffle your day? Such loads of stuff
to dump or recycle at the end of the day!

No one's better than our Friend in the Kitchen to sort out all that material in our heads and hearts. He knows where we've been – or not been. He knows what we have done . . . or not done. He knows how we've reacted to every circumstance. He not only knows, he cares.

The close of day is a good time to review with our Friend the collection that's accumulated in our minds and hearts. He is willing and able to help recycle, compost or dump our stuff wisely and well. You need only ask!

Windows

The window in my kitchen faces south.
That's great, for when the sun shines,
the kitchen's bright and cheerful, and
that lifts the spirits. Contrariwise, it's
not so great, in that, when working, the
sun blinds me!

Don't you feel sorry for kitchens without
a window? No fresh air, not to mention a
view. My window's interesting in that
there's movement in the road outside,
including noises of life and living. It's not
the most beautiful prospect, but then
looking out of the window is not the
reason I'm in it.

The tale is told of a woman who worked in a kitchen whose window looked out onto several back gardens either side of her own. Sounds very pleasant, doesn't it? But Hilda grumbled about the washing on the line of her next-door-but-one neighbour.

'Can't think how a young woman like her has got the nerve to hang out such grey-looking washing! I'd be ashamed of it if it were mine!'

One morning Hilda was moaning to another friend about the grey washing – again. There they sat, looking out on to the well-tended gardens, where the offending laundry blew merrily in the breeze. 'Hilda,' asked the neighbour, ' when did you last clean your windows?'

Oops!

Once Hilda's windows were cleaned, she was surprised to see how much whiter and brighter her young neighbour's washing became.

Hilda and you and I cannot see clearly through grey and greasy glass. As one optician likes to quip, 'You can't be optimistic if you have a misty optic.'

It really does help to be sure that we're not blinkered when we gaze at 'a neighbour's washing'. As our Friend put it when he talked with his friends in Galilee, 'Take the branch out of your own eye before you offer to take a splinter out of anyone else's.' Today he asks us to make sure our windows are sparkly clean before we look out of them. His original super window-cleaner is ours for the asking – free. It's called . . .

God's love.

Floors

One especially interesting kitchen floor I've walked on was made with large Phoenician flagstones. They were brought over from Phoenicia to Cornwall and were traded for cargoes of tin. The fascination of this kitchen lies in the legend that a wealthy businessman, Joseph of Arimathea, visited here on business trips from Phoenicia!

Today, the kitchens that come with houses and flats often have too little room to swing a cat, barely enough wall space to place all the mod cons, and just about enough floor space for cook to stand in the middle of it. By reaching up, down, sideways to left or right, or swivelling through 90°, Mum is able to prepare, cook and serve a family meal. Aren't mums wonderful?

119

Now kitchen floors need cleaning, and I'm grateful for the one that came with my house. It's small, it's not flagstone but vinyl, so it's easily maintained. There are several ways to do this. One is to use a squeegee mop, another is to get down on your knees and scrub, and then there's my way. Drop a damp cloth on to the floor, wiggle it around with one foot as far as possible over the floor. Rotate as necessary while clutching the kitchen sink with one hand and the worktop with the other. Pick up the messy cloth while still clutching the sink, and wash it. Meanwhile make sure no one is around to see you do this.

I know – my way's not a good way. Not everyone will agree with my choice of the best way either, that is, to get down on your knees. It's easier to cope with crevices and corners while down there.

'Satan trembles when he sees the weakest saint upon her knees', so keep him trembling while you scrub. Talk to your ever-listening Friend about your concerns, physical or spiritual. Ask him for ideas to bring zest to your daily life, for words to encourage another. Or perhaps . . .

Just listen. . . . Hear him speak to you.

Redecorating

Eventually kitchens need redecorating, sometimes even remodelling, and that's an opportunity to indulge designer dreams. Redecorating comes with less enthusiasm perhaps. There's an air of 'we've done this before and it's a bother' attitude. A way has to be found to scrape, clean and paint around, or move, the cooker, the fridge-freezer, the washing machine, the dishwasher and who knows what else. Even the amount of muscle available for said tasks needs consideration.

In my case a 'clean and freshen up' was
what my kitchen needed. Its pristine
glow gone, sunshine was showing up
smudges, spots and plaster cracks. So
along comes The Boss to take a look,
followed by his mate with the steps,
brushes and paint. The work began, and
the men were left to it.

All went smoothly, according to plan. Yet on returning home several hours later, my home seemed strangely quiet – until I reached the kitchen. There behind the door was a very vocal and frustrated Boss! Mate had gone on an errand, and while he was gone, The Boss found that the handle on the closed door refused to budge. He was locked in the kitchen for a good thirty minutes and it was another thirty before his lively sense of humour rose to the occasion. Then he set about finding and fixing a new lock!

It's likely that all of us have been locked in, locked out or locked up at some time or other. Quite frightening and claustrophobic no doubt it was, too. Maybe the locking was physical; maybe it was being locked into a difficult time in life. The helplessness of being excluded from the world around you is so hard to endure or even understand.

It's hard not to panic!

No matter how frustrating or frightening
the lock-up, our Friend is there with you.
He never leaves to run an errand. If you
find that thought hard to accept, next
time you find yourself in a tight spot,
try talking to him anyway.
He's listening, always.

You might even find he's handing
you the key to the lock!

'I've found a Friend, oh, such a Friend,
So kind, and true and tender,
So wise a Counsellor and Guide,
So mighty a Defender!
From him who loves me now so well,
What powers my soul can sever?
Shall life? or death? or earth? or Hell?
No! I am his forever.'

James G. Small

Kitchen closed

due to

gas failure!